Murmurations

a collection of
poems

Vic Blake

Murmurations
© Vic Blake 2022

www.vicblakewriter.co.uk

The right of the author to be identified as the author of this work
has been asserted in accordance with the
Copyright, Designs and Patents Act 1988.

All rights reserved.
No part of this publication may be reproduced, stored in a retrieval system, or transmitted, in any form or by any means, electronic, mechanical, photocopying, recording or otherwise, without the prior permission of the copyright owners.

ISBN 978-1-910779-88-0 (Paperback)

Typeset by
Oxford eBooks Ltd.
www.oxford-ebooks.com

Front Cover Design: Vic Blake
Front Cover Photograph: Michael Luck

It is my delight to dedicate this volume to Maggie, my ever-patient wife, and to my two sons and four grandchildren, all of whom I love beyond mere words.

Table of Contents

Introduction	8
Crocodile	12
Pussy Cat	14
Easy Peasy	16
Humpty Dumpty	17
There Once Was a Woman Called Myrtle	17
Ali Was an Alligator	18
Starkle, Starkle Little Twink	18
Tea Time by the Nile	19
I Lost my Watch	20
The One-Legged Man	21
Sunset Over Welwyn, 1969	22
A Little Matter of Pride	24
Would That I Were a Morris Dancer	26
The Ballad of DIY Dave	28
Funny Boo Hoo!	30
Mr Fixit	31
Baptism	33
Never Smile at a Crocodile	36
Cock-a-doodle Moo	36
The Very Rude Note	38
Never Upset a Poet	45
Mind the Gap	46
The Space	48
Somebody Pulled My Plug Out	50
Ode To Gin and Orange	53
A Man Whose Name I Forget	54
A Colleague of Volatile Mood	54
Down Under our Stairs	55

The West Wind	62
Love On a String	63
The Body Politic	65
Galicia	67
Shit Happens	70
Ping-pong	72
Missing You	74
Old Dog	75
Sky	77
Hanging On	78
He Handed Me a Poem	80
The Winding Road	82
Bananas	83
Worm	84
Buridan's Ass	86
See-through Glasses	87
Spyder, Spyder	89
Il Italiano	91
Sparrow	94
Pond	95
Sonnet to a Minor Stroke	97
Alive and Creaking	98
An Autumn Muse	100
Last Words to a Dear Friend	101
February, Somewhere in the North of England	103
A Day Called Night	105
Omicron	107
All in a Jumblie	108
Letter to Santa	112
Girly Swat	115
On Growing Old	116
To the Wind a Seed	118
Nuggets of Gold	119

For Little Arthur	120
Villanelle for an Ageing Socialist	121
Seasonal Haikus	123
Twenty-Twenty Hindsight	124
Beware the Ignoramus	125
The Day I Found a Frog in Our Toilet	127
Poetry Read in a Silly Voice	128
Not Raving but Clowning	129
A 'Real Man' Declares his Love	130
Thingummyjig	131
About the Author	132

Introduction

I must begin by saying that I never really considered myself to be 'A Poet' at all, not in any serious sense of the word anyway – and, never having had any kind of literary education, I confess to only the most cursory knowledge of literature and poetry in general. But, like so many other ordinary workaday 'bods', I would scribble the odd few lines of verse here and there, from time to time, only then to put them away in a file somewhere that was all-too-easy to forget. In this way, years might roll by with little more to speak of than a few assorted jottings, disembodied ideas and half-finished pieces. And that might have been the end of it were it not for Covid and my asthma and my resultant almost complete lockdown during 2020/21.

There is surely nothing like a protracted confinement to concentrate the mind in the direction of a 'project' of some kind. So, freshly-motivated, I revisited my jottings, saw what I thought might be a certain potential, tried some of this out on friends and was delighted by their reaction, and out of this the initial idea for a book of poetry was born (as well as a collection of short stories and a now, half-written novel). Having then sorted through what I had, I knew I was going to have to do some serious editing and then to complete a lot more writing before I had anything like a 'Collection' to speak of. If nothing else, the exercise helped to keep me sane.

Thus, while many of the earlier pieces go back several decades, to my time as a teacher and even beyond, there is a lot of my more recent writing in here as well.

Organising it all was another matter. While earlier poems and those on the theme of childhood tend to appear near the beginning, and more recent poems, including those pertaining to my galloping old age, appear mostly towards the end, I have resisted the temptation (not very successfully) to organise these into any strict temporal order.

Taken as a whole, the collection reflects on the eternal themes of love and loss, lessons learned, childhood, parenthood and ageing, and so on, including my personal thoughts on gender and on men and masculinity in particular. Others take a more humorous look at life just for its own sake, while some are sad or even tragic, some vaguely philosophical, and others simple light-hearted and playful nonsense. And then there are those that take a well-deserved swipe at some of the absurdities and iniquities of life as well as at those who inflict them upon the rest of us. I have also included a couple of songs here, more for their message than any strict poetic value, though I am fascinated by the awkwardness of turning poetry into song, and vice versa. In several cases, too, I have added brief notes by way of context.

But why crocodiles feature so often in my poetry is a question I am happy to leave to the reader.

These first three poems were written in April 1986 towards the end of a very difficult period in my life during which I was also recovering from a serious accident which had put me out of work for well over a year.

Back at work once more, now as a part-time supply teacher, I wrote these for the amusement of the pupils of St. Luke's School, Loughton, where they brought so much warmth and sunshine back into my life.

I wonder if any of them still remember me! And I wonder if anyone still has a copy of the school magazine that a couple of them were originally published in.

The seven poems that follow on from these were also written, at various times, for children.

Crocodile

I took the kids for a swim today;
    Debbie, Sharon, Troy,
David, and Susan with the cut toe,
    and several more excited,
plotting-to-duck-Sir kids from
    another class,
all thoroughly determined to have fun
    in the water.

We walked in a long crocodile
    across the road and
down the long hill,
    past nodding daffodils and the
neatly laid lawns of
    plush suburban homes,
blindly opulent,
    quarter-of-a-million pound
        (How much is a million Sir?)
    ever-so-desirable residences.
Then the crocodile began to limp
    like me, rocking comically
to one side until, helpless, it
    chuckled itself to pieces.

At the poolside it looked
    safe enough.
They hooted, they waved, they smiled
    (but then crocodiles always do)
and they begged me into

   the giggling water
with their winked reassurances and
   seal pup charm.

They were upon me, of course,
   in an instant.
I was dragged under thrashing,
   tussled by Troy,
savaged by Sharon,
   splashed unremittingly
and horribly abused,
   and all in the name
      of fun.

But I didn't mind really,
   It's very important – fun.
It turns lists into people,
   schools into places
where kids like to be,
   crocodiles into bath-mates.

Pussy Cat

Once a big black pussycat
Underneath a big tree sat
And watched a little dickie bird,
Sweetest thing he'd ever heard.
See the pussy sitting there,
See the birdie, unaware.
Hear that birdie, *tweet, tweet, chirp;*
Watch that pussy, *munch, munch, burp!*

From deep down in that pussy's tum
A beauteous singing then did come.
No matter what that pussy did,
Where he ran or where he hid,
That birdie tweeted out its tune
So loud and shrill that, very soon,
The other pussies overheard
And thought that Pussy was a bird.

How they chased him round and round.
How they loved that birdie sound,
Thinking such a lovely song
To a great big blackbird must belong.
'It must have fallen from that tree!
How delicious! Goodness me!'
They chased him over distant hills
And, for all we know, he's running still.

So be careful, kind and wise
And pick on people your own size.
Remember that poor pussy cat,
Oh so very big and fat,
How he came to wish that he
Had left that birdie in its tree:
All little people have their days
And get you back in subtle ways.

Easy Peasy

Easy Peasy,
Japanezy,
lemon squeezy,
bread and cheesy,
birds and beesy,
cough and sneezy,
hands and kneesy,
dogs and fleasy,
apple treesy,
it's so easy,
just continue
as you pleasey.

Humpty Dumpty

Humpty Dumpty sat on a wall,
Humpty Dumpty had a great fall.
All the King's horses
And all the King's men said,
His mum must have been
An extremely big hen!

There Once Was a Woman Called Myrtle

There once was a woman called Myrtle
Who entered a race with a turtle,
She thought he'd be slow
But he couldn't half go
As off like a rocket he hurtled.

Ali Was an Alligator

Ali was an alligator,
Took a job as a wine bar waiter,
Met a girl and asked to date her,
Took her out and two days later,
Ali alligator ate 'er.

Starkle, Starkle Little Twink

Starkle, starkle, little twink,
How I wonder what you drink,
Is it coffee? Is it tea?
It's a mystery to me.
Starkle, starkle little twink –
I am dafter than you think!

Tea Time by the Nile

Croc-croc-crocodile ,
Basking by the River Nile,
I watched you
And you watched me,
And I saw you croco-smile.

Saus-saus-sausages,
How I love them for my tea.
You, though,
I can plainly see,
Would rather make a meal of me.

Lying there, your croco-claws
Fix you on all croco-fours
While great, white
Croco-fearsome teeth
Flash back at me from gaping jaws.

Croc-croc-crocodile,
Basking by the River Nile,
I think I just might go and stand
Somewhere safer for a while!

I Lost my Watch

I lost my watch the other day,
Put it somewhere safe, away
From all the dust and dirt and grime.

If I could, I'm bound to say,
I'd look for it again today,
But I no longer have the time.

So I hope, on Christmas Day,
Another one might come my way,
To replace that missing watch of mine.

For in the end, and come what may,
It's very true, what they all say;
There is no present like the time.

The One-Legged Man

One warm and sunny morning,
The air so clear and still,
I met a man with one leg
Hopping up a hill.

The hill was high and very steep,
It was all that I could do
To reach the top with two good legs
To see the splendid view.

It would take me many hours,
For him, though, many more,
So I asked him why he did it,
For his leg was getting sore.

'I have to reach the top', he said.
'But why?' I asked with a frown.
'Because,' he said, 'it's so much fun
When I roll back down'.

Sunset Over Welwyn, 1969

Twilight,
The peaceful hour,
The sleepy eye,
The closing flower
That bows its head in petal-white
Prayer before the coming night.

As the soft light fades,
Those gentle hues
Of coral pinks
And smoky blues
Slowly change, now to take
The form of an immense sky-lake
Of molten golds
And fiery reds,
That glowing, swirling,
Bathes the heads
Of silent lovers,
Lying still,
Breathless
In their single will.

And in some quiet
And secret place,
Two lovers touch
each other's face...
The sun goes down
As they embrace.

This is the earliest poem in this collection, written soon after I came out of the army and before I set off on my travels. At that time I was just a lonely young man, longing for love but entirely lacking in the confidence to make it happen.

A Little Matter of Pride

What was *that!*
I gasped,
stifling my laughter
with mock surprise.
It was a bum burp,
you replied…
such satisfaction in your eyes!
Laughing loudly like a drain,
your chest puffed up with little-boy pride,
I struggled to push my mischievous thoughts
back down again and to one side.

Well…
I said, twinkling,
as down we sat,
don't you let Grandma
hear you do that.
But the idea was out
and I could no longer keep
the thought or the laughter
under my hat.

Something so innocent –
A little boy's fart –
awoke in me
some forgotten flame
of childish mischief,
deep down in my own heart.

And, oh… how,
with all my grown-up decorum,
I wished
I could be little again
Right now.

I wrote this for my first son, Yugen, when he was very young, and we lived under the ever-judgmental and persecutory gaze of the mother-in-law from Hell.

Would That I Were a Morris Dancer

Would that I were a morris dancer,
With a hey and a ho
And a hey, nonny no.
Would that I could dance at all,
Strip-the-willow, jive and tango,
I would have me such a ball,
With a hey and a nonny nay no.

Would that I could chase the lasses,
With a hey and a ho
And a hey nonny no.
Would that I could run at all,
Over the hills and through the heather,
I would love them one and all,
With a hey and a nonny nay no.

Would that I could climb that mountain,
With a hey and a ho
And a hey nonny no.
Would that I'd the strength at all,
I'd shade my eyes to the far horizon
And follow where my heart would call,
With a hey and a nonny nay no.

Would that it were springtime always,
With a hey and a ho
And a hey, nonny no.
Would that it were spring at all,
I'd rise up with the sun each morning
And not stop singing till I'd seen it fall,
With a hey and a nonny nay no.

I wrote this poem while I was recovering from a terrible accident in which I was hit, head on, by an oncoming car. At first they were unsure whether or not I might lose my right foot. When I was told that they could save it, they informed me that walking would always be difficult and probably painful. And things would likely get worse. It goes without saying that dancing, like walking in the hills, would be out of the question from here on. There is also more than a hint here of how depleted I felt, particularly, as I imagined at the time, in the eyes of the opposite sex.

The Ballad of DIY Dave

What can be so hard
about doing it yourself,
sanding down those floorboards
or putting up that shelf!
Anyone could do it
with just an ounce of wit,
a careful eye, a steady hand,
and the right tools in your kit,

plus a modicum of knowhow
gleaned from the internet,
and a super-duper power drill,
the best that you can get.
And look at all the dosh you save
when you DIY;
no more hefty builders' bills
to bleed the coffers dry.

And when those brand new shelves collapse
and the wife begins to cry,
I'll simply reassure her:
I'll get to it by and by,
once the football's finished
and Sunday comes around
and I've squandered all our hard-earned cash
on some new gizmo that I found.

Then watch me fix that leaking tap,
mend that broken chair,
demolish that dividing wall
and sort that creaky stair.
Then you'll see what I can do!
Stand back and watch me fly,
your handyman *extraordinaire*,
your king of DIY.

Funny Boo Hoo!

Funny how life goes awry sometimes,
Like it's all been too easy by far.
Then the problems crowd round
Like wolves at your door,
And I don't mean, 'funny *ha ha*'!

Funny how life rolls on like a dream,
As though somehow it's all meant to fool you.
Then it all goes wrong and crumbles to dust,
And I don't mean 'funny *peculiar*'!

Funny, I was once so complacent.
There was nothing I couldn't do,
Till one day my world turned upside down,
Funny that…
'*Funny boo, hoo*'!

Mr Fixit

It is the middle of the night.
It is oven hot
and the soft hiss of distant traffic
pours in through the open window
with the sweet-scented honeysuckle breeze.

You have kicked off your sheets
and smell like baking bread as I watch you
sipping at sleep like cream soda.
And I think back, tearful, on the times when,
cast in the role of breadwinner, provider,
tap-and-toy-mender, decision maker, general
Mr. Fixit
and, worst of all, disciplinarian,
I lashed out,
wild like a cobra
when the strain of it all became too much.

Now, my lovely boy, I fear that
I have fixed you
and your children to be, just as my father
fixed me,
as though in that flash of anger
we transmit a contagious disease that
destroys understanding, stultifies reason
and rots the heart…
The bee stings
and then dies itself.

I want so much to wake you now,
to hug you, love you,
beg your forgiveness,
unfixit,
but you need your sleep
and I know
you wouldn't really understand.

To Yugen.

Baptism

It is nothing to him,
a mere scrap of paper,
worthless, contemptible,
not even fit for the bin,
while I, like a war-blasted child,
watch my entire world
erupt in flames before me.

Aghast, my knees wobble
as I watch my masterpiece
writhe, wriggle and scream
its short, innocent life away
in the molten red mouth
of the fearsome hearth,
curling and twisting in on itself
in one final, desperate,
hopeless, agonising gesture,
to shield its precious treasure
from the angry heat,
the red heat,
the all-consuming
murderous
fire.

With searing pain
and jaw-dropping disbelief
I watch the brown creep quickly
across the white page,
curl to the black, until suddenly,

like demons,
the jagged yellow flames leap up
to scream their prize;
terrible spark,
stab and crackle fire,
a thousand frenzied cannibals,
wild dance in bright red plumage,
cackling their mad song;
Burn the beast!
Kill the beast!
Eat the beast –
my lovely, colourful,
beautiful friend.

Through a kaleidoscope of
shards and splinters, big, blue,
blobbing, sobbing tears,
I stand and watch, numb,
helpless, crying;
'*Why*, Daddy, *Why*' tears,
choking, pleading,
My drawing, Daddy.
My very best ever drawing, Daddy.
I am right there, in that drawing,
Daddy.
Look!
Look!
Just there,
just in front of the volcano,
a gun in my hand,
see!
there!
Killing all the baddies, Daddy.
Daddy!

And now I too am fire, Daddy!
I am heat,
Daddy!
Red heat,
white hot heat, unstoppable,
murderous heat,
just like those wild cannibals,
just like *You*,
Daddy!

Here I offer a glimpse into my own childhood with an early memory of an extraordinarily difficult father. He was volatile and unpredictable and really quite savage in the ways that he would put down his children. It was a lifetime's work learning how to get over him.

Never Smile at a Crocodile

Never smile at a crocodile,
Though his expression may beguile,
He will surely draw you in a while,
Into that all-consuming smile.

Better, in true cowards' style,
To run a very rapid mile!

Cock-a-doodle Moo

Cock-a-doodle-moo,
Whatever shall I do,
My father was a chicken
and my mother was a coo!

The veterinary said,
I cannae do a lot the noo…
but could ye manage me a dozen eggs
and a pint of milk or two?

I actually wrote this poem almost entirely in my sleep. The Milliganesque title was the beginning and simply appeared later in a dream and hung around to play with me for a while.

The Scottish accent owes much to my many close friendships with those from north of the border, Maggie, my wife, being but one of them at that time.

The Very Rude Note

Once upon a summer's day,
Long ago and far away,
A teacher sat and worked his way
Through a pile of half-marked books
While casting the occasional look
Around the class assembled there,
To show them he was still aware.

Thus the lesson murmured by
Till something chanced to catch his eye,
But doing little, save to stare
A moment at the giggling pair,
He went back to his marking stint,
Imagining they might take the hint.

A little later on, however,
The twosome, being none too clever,
Returned once more to their little caper,
Passing on their piece of paper.
Then, as the stifled laughter spread,
The giggling and the straining heads,

So interest in the note increased
Till very soon all writing ceased
As eager pupils begged to see
The cause of the hilarity,
Grinning, puzzled, pained and vexed,
Each one pleading to be next.

Now, in the clamour that prevailed,
And realising his ploy had failed,
The teacher looked up from his books
And saw the pleading, plaintive looks
And, where two red-faced girls were seated,
Something hurriedly secreted.

Gesturing with outstretched hand
He issued forth a stern command
To bring whatever it might be
Down to the front for him to see.
But hastily the note was passed
From lap to lap across the class,

While on each pupils countenance
That practised look of innocence,
The degree of which he knew to be
The measure of their trickery,
So up he got and made his way
To where a certain schoolbag lay.

Its owner duly reprimanded,
He stressed the item should be handed
Over to him straight away
Or else there would be hell to pay,
At which the boy's face went so red
He had to help himself instead.

The class fell now to a deathly hush.
He could almost hear their faces blush
As he opened up the crumpled note
And felt the lump come to his throat,
For its detailed contents, now inspected,
Were not at all what he'd expected.

Depicted there for all to see
Were scenes of such debauchery,
Shenanigans which were so lewd
They far surpassed the merely rude.
Yet there was more, at which he froze
As his glasses slipped from off his nose.

Not a titter could he hear.
Never before in all his years,
With all that he had seen and heard,
Had he ever been so lost for words.
Eyes agape, mouth agaper,
He stared aghast at the piece of paper

While expectantly the class looked on,
Every spark of humour gone,
For they, like he, had recognised
The object of his stunned surprise
Entangled there with several other
Ample and contorted lovers.

Five or six there were, at least,
Some fruit and veg and an ape-like beast
Unknown to zoological science,
Plus a vacuum cleaner-like appliance,
All put to such imaginative use
By the teacher in his welly boots!

Now, although he had no pimple there,
There was no mistaking that thinning hair,
Those horn-rimmed glasses, the bulbous waist...
This really was in the poorest taste,
Flattering in but one respect –
And that to startling effect!

But what to do, he wasn't sure.
Several hundred lines or more
Were warranted, there was no doubt,
But should the news of this leak out,
What then? He'd be the perfect fool,
The laughing stock of all the school,

A walking joke, nobody
Would ever take him seriously
Again. No! He'd simply have to try
Some other way of rectifying –
Talented though they might be –
This slur upon his dignity.

He stood and pondered for a while
Then, suddenly, began to smile,
For all at once, of course, he knew
The very thing that he should do,
A simple, yet effective way
To make the blighters rue the day
They'd ever hatched their little plan.
No butt of children's jokes this man!

For a bit of an artist too was he,
A dab hand with the old H.B.!

One or two who sat close by
Caught the twinkle in his eye,
The flash of mischief in his face
As he turned and strolled back to his place
Down at the front, back at his chair,
Where he sat back down with a devilish air.

There, at his desk, his pupils saw
Him open up his left-hand drawer
And on his face, as he searched therein,
The look in his eye and the fiendish grin
That sent a shiver round the room,
Like some portent of impending doom.

All looked on now with anxious faces,
Quietly fidgeting in their places,
For on his desk, where his books had been,
Paper and pencils could now be seen.
Then, having sharpened three or four,
He cracked his knuckles and looked up once more,
And the penny dropped…
And they knew the score.

Now, being an observant kind of teacher,
With an eye for detail and those finer features,
He scrutinised their guilty faces
And, with squinting eye, picked out those traces
That make each individual child unique;
The smart, the funny, the cocky, the meek,
The playground bully and the 'hide-and-seek',

All yielded to his artist's gaze,
Divulged their secrets and their little ways,
As his pencil moved, once engaged,
Like a thing demented around the page,
Pausing for detail, just once in a while,
Making him chuckle, raising a smile
As inscrutable as any crocodile.

This fresh demeanour they now saw
Unhinged his pupils all the more,
And as he sketched, so they squirmed,
Their worst imaginings now confirmed
About their teacher and all those rumours
About his wicked sense of humour.

Gone now every trace of fun
As he sketched their faces, one by one,
While they, in their self-conscious hell,
Prayed for the end-of-lesson bell,
Keen to leave, yet desperate to see
The end results of his artistry.
For none could bear to leave behind
The work of such a devious mind.

At the bell, on their way to the door,
They begged him and pleaded, cajoled and implored
Him to show them his artwork, desperate that he
Should put them out of their misery.
But all of his sketches, now put away,
Would never again see the light of day,
But gather dust on some high shelf,
The exercise being the end in itself.

From that day onwards things went well.
And, though none grew wings, all could tell
That a sense of calm had been restored.
And should they again get restless or bored,
The artists among them would know their place,
Their pencils stay zipped up in their case,
No more to be used with such reckless haste.

In the end it was they who sealed their fate
As the original artist, so quiet of late,
Yet so creative by inclination,
Fell victim to his own imagination.
What would happen, he confided,
If eventually he decided
That those drawings we have never seen,
Should appear one day in the school magazine!

Where wild lampoonery once held sway,
A mild paranoia now ruled the day.
So all agreed and considered it best
To quietly let the matter rest,
Not to provoke him, keep him sweet,
Keep their antics more downbeat.

And as for the artist, who was of course
The inspiration and the source
Of all that merriment and all that fun,
They broke his pencils, every one!

I started writing this during my teaching days, when I first began to practice writing poetry, often during long and tedious spells of exam invigilation. In fact it sat around for three decades after that until I got round to finishing it off.

Never Upset a Poet

Never upset a poet
For he'll take your ill-spent words
And turn them into serpents
And crocodiles, and birds.
And serpents may constrict your heart,
And crocodiles may bite,
And birds may fly around your head
So you cannot sleep at night.

Be mindful of the poet
For the poet stands apart,
And sees the magic of this world
In the beating of our hearts.
He'll find the words that we cannot,
Whole worlds within a flower,
And sunshine on the darkest days
To light our lonely hours.

And should you love a poet
He will take your mundane things
And turn them into butterflies
On brightly-coloured wings.
He will cup your heart in loving hands
Like a tiny fledgling bird,
And let fly a murmuration
Of a thousand loving words.

Mind the Gap

What's it like to be you? he said,
My classmate on that cloudy day.
We'd been in the playground, kicking a ball
And the bell had gone for the end of play
When he popped the question, just like that,
Not even really looking at me,
But my head went *pop* and my ears went deaf,
I was lost for words and could hardly see.

And I stood, stock-still, at the foot of the steps,
That led up to the door, that led into the school,
As children pushed past me, all elbows and knees
While I mouthed like a goldfish and gawked like a fool.
How could I answer a question like that!
My thoughts were like fireworks in my head
And, though I tried my best to speak,
No sounds would come and no words were said.

I was hardly nine and yet, since then,
I've thought long and hard, though I still have no clue
How you could know what it's like to be me
Or how I could know what it's like to be you.
But now I am older and have learned certain things
About people and life and the power of the heart
And how, through love, we can learn to cross
That great void that keeps us so far apart.

Another true story, based on an incident from my own school days, a memory that was simply too good not to write about. My friend's name was Raymond, a tall gangly boy whose eccentricities, I know, rubbed off on me. I very much doubt that he remembers this or the effect it had on me.

The Space

There is a space,
Somewhere
Between the moment and the mile,
Between the dream and the anvil,
Between you and me,
A space so vast
It is bigger than a baby,
Wider than its smile,
Longer than its heartbeat,
Deeper than its gaze,
As deep as the love
I still feel for you.

In that space the ages roll on
Timelessly like breakers,
Forever breaking,
Always crashing,
Never mending.

In that space
Dreams become lost
And I can no longer
Find my way.
Where *do* you go
When up is down,
And when left is right,
And when there is no way
Either in or out.

In that space
It is so very cold,
Though we kid each other not.
Instead we pull on another layer
And cover our ears,
Trying not to hear
Those faint, distant echoes of
All that love, all those dreams
Gone so slowly,
So surely by.

In that space my trickling life
Wears down my dreams,
As smooth as a stone,
Washes away my longings
And my reason for being.
Watch as it all
Disappears into the ether
Like a sigh, like a kiss,
Barely remembered,
From long,
Long ago…
But say
Nothing!

Somebody Pulled My Plug Out

Somebody pulled my plug out
While I wasn't looking,
And suddenly I am deflated
Like last night's party balloon,
Wrinkled, saggy, jaded,
Pointless,
I neither bounce nor float
But lollop about the house,
A featureless entity,
Drifting, flopping
Into odd corners,
Untidy,
Un-loved…
So it seems.

Kick me now,
I won't bounce,
Play with me,
I won't oblige.
Prick me,
I won't pop,
Any breath I contain
Serves little purpose now,
Save half-heartedly
To prop up this limp skin.

I make no children laugh,
Nobody merry,
No room brighter,

Though I do take up less space
Than yesterday,
Which is something I suppose.

Later I shall climb lead-footed
The slow stairs to my bed
Where I know, as my head falls
Through the pillow,
I shall leave these dismal feelings
Far behind me.

Into playful sleep then
I shall pass,
Through the looking glass
Of my torment,
Up and away from
The jagged shards and
The spiteful fragments of
This Alice-world,
Into a moving collage of
Harmless nonsense and
Potty frivolities,
And where,
With a little bit of luck,
I shall look to the sky and,
With one great
Wonderful leap,
Fly skywards once more.

In writing this piece I was reminded of the helpful distinction to be made between common human misery, that we all go through once in a while, and actual depression. The one is a natural and understandable response to adverse circumstances while the latter often has a persistent inner component which is far harder to recognise and pin down, let alone to overcome, and it can seem to come out of nowhere and at any time.

Ode To Gin and Orange

Every evening I look forward
To a nice cold gin and orange.
Coming home from work I'm smiling'
With anticipation for in
Just a short while I know well
That in my kitchen I'll be pourin'
Generous amounts of gin
To enhance the flavour of that foreign
Juice that we all love so well,
The always scrummy, never borin',
Just amazing, quite delicious,
Universal cure for snorin',
Jaffa, Florida – in short,
The sweet, delightful, lovely orange.

A Man Whose Name I Forget

A man, whose name I forget,
Stole everything that he could get.
He once took a shine to an item of mine,
A decision he'll always regret.

A Colleague of Volatile Mood

A colleague of volatile mood
Was extremely officious and rude.
I was getting uptight
Till I saw her one night
Dancing outside in the nude.

Down Under our Stairs

Down in the dark cellar
Under our stairs,
Deep under our stairs,
In the spidery black,
Where it's blacker than black,
No-one will go,
For no-one would dare,
Where cobwebs and spiders
All covered in hair
Lurk in the corners
And wait to ensnare
Any foolish child
Who might venture down there.

I was told that a child
Once did venture down there,
Down under our stairs,
In the dust and the gloom,
The impenetrable gloom.
He just unlocked the door
And opened it wide
And then, feeling his way,
Walked slowly inside
And right to the bottom
Where horrid things hide
That jump out and bite you
And slither and slide.

For down there in the dark,
Deep under our stairs,
Far under the stairs,
Live all manner of things,
Hideous things!
Yet down there he went
With hardly a care,
Down into the monsters'
Bone-littered lair,
Where they scratched him and bit him
And pulled out his hair,
And he never again
Came back out of there.

And sometimes, if you listen,
In the still of the night,
In the dark of the night,
When all are asleep,
In their warm, cosy sleep,
You might just hear faint noises –
If nobody snores –
A low, mournful growling,
The scratching of claws,
And the grinding of teeth
In those big hungry jaws,
Deep down in our cellar,
Behind those locked doors.

That's why, in our house,
Nearly everyone's scared,
They're all well aware
Of what lurks in that cellar,
That awful dark cellar,

Behind padlocked doors,
Down under our stairs,
Where fierce things wait
To grab you unawares
And pull you down with them
By the legs and the hair
And eat you all up
Till your bones are stripped bare.

Except for our Maisie!
She doesn't care…
She never did care,
About spiders and monsters,
Even big scary monsters,
Hungry and dribbling
In the dark down there,
In the depths of our cellar,
Down under our stairs,
Not even the snakes
And the huge grizzly bears,
That could bite off your head
Like a juicy ripe pear.

Then one day she went looking
For her lost teddy bear,
Her sweet teddy bear,
With its curly brown hair,
That was missing somewhere.
And in a moment's despair…

She went down to the cellar
And unlocked the padlock,
That big, heavy padlock,
Made of cold shiny steel,
The hardest of steel,
And she opened the door,
Her torch by her side,
And from the top of the steps
She straight away spied
Those cold, yellow eyes,
Hungry and wide,
In pairs, staring back at her,
From the darkness inside.

For a moment she stood
At the top of the steps,
The cold stone steps,
And peered down inside
To where horrid things hide.
Then she stepped down into
The darkness within,
While the monsters they waited
With big, hungry grins,
So close now they could smell
Her soft warm skin.
Drooling and wiping
The spit from their chins,

They got ready to grab her
As she slowly came closer,
Closer, and closer,
Almost in reach…
So nearly in reach!

Then one monster leapt up
With a deafening 'Roaaaaaaaar!'
And it reached out to grab her
With its needle-sharp claws
And the others joined in
With their great snapping jaws,
But then…
'Stop that!' said Maisie,
And everything paused.

The monsters fell silent
While Maisie she waited,
Stared back and waited,
Not at all cross,
For she knew who was boss!
And it wasn't these 'monsters',
No matter how scary,
How scaly or hungry,
Or horrid or hairy.
And now it was they
Who were frightened and wary
Of this sweet little girl
With her manner so airy.

'I have something to tell you,'
She eventually said,
With a toss of her head
And a look in her eyes
That was gentle and wise,
While the monsters they listened
With quiet fascination
As she told them the story
Of their own creation

In the minds of young children
From past generations,
With their young, overactive
Imaginations.

And when she had finished
The monsters were sad,
So terribly sad.
And they hugged one another,
And then, one after the other,
Said goodbye to Maisie
And went on their way,
Wiping their eyes
I'm so sad to say,
Back into the shadows
And far, far away.
And then Maisie – and her teddy
Came back out to play.

I wrote this still very much with children in mind. It also taps into particular memories from my own childhood of dark spidery places and those adult stories I was told of being locked in the coal hole as naughty children. In particular I remember the fearsome 'Bogey Hole' as being a special place of immeasurable fear and dread.

Three songs: the first about men's all-too-common fear of commitment; the second about how badly it can go wrong, should we ever commit to the wrong person, and the third a political broadside – volunteers most welcome.

The West Wind

Song

They say that four winds blow
And I have followed three,
Now I hear the west wind calling me.
Even though I love you so,
The time has come and I must go and see
Why the west wind keeps on calling me.

You know I told you,
When I first breezed into town,
That I could never hope to settle down.
All my searching high and low
Meant that I would only let you down,
Stop my feet from landing on the ground.

They say that I will never really know my mind,
That somehow all my looking made me blind.
Travelling light the open road
Left me with a heavy load, you see,
A slave to my own longing to be free.

And when I hear your voice
Come whispering down the wind,
The rain outside bring on the rain within,
Loneliness, my only friend,
Right up to the bitter end will be,
Till the north wind calls to set me free.

Love On a String
Song

Love on a string, love on a string,
You had me like a yo-yo.
Oh how I rue counting on you,
You made me feel so low.
One day I'm up, next day I'm down,
Live my life in a spin,
Knowing you keep your love on a string.

Once I would bring, love on the wing,
Fly to you like a sparrow,
Each day a little closer to you,
So far from the straight and narrow.
You had me eating out of your hand,
I didn't suspect a thing.
I just couldn't see your love on a string.

Once I would fling care to the wind,
High as a kite I'm flying.
The harder she pulls, the higher I go,
But always this cold wind sighing.
One hand I see waving to me,
The other so tightly clings.
Why do you keep your love on a string?

So now I sing, love on a string,
Given away so freely,
And oh what a prize, the light in your eyes,
If only my friends could see me!

But just when I feel that this is for real
You just go and reel it in.
Why do you keep your love on a string?
Why do you keep your love on a string?

The Body Politic
Song

When I die, as die I must,
Not for me a plot of dust,
Nor reduced to ash in some
Soul-less crematorium.
Let me, when I run out of breath,
Take retribution in my death
Upon the bastards who, in life,
Caused such sorrow, grief and strife.

So gather round and hear my plan,
Come on friends and lend a hand
And take a swipe at all those who
Ministered or voted blue.
Among the tory seats of power
This simple soul will have his hour.
A voting life did me no good,
So listen now and listen good.

Strip me naked, lay me bare,
With super-glue my thumb prepare,
Palm outstretched in mocking pose,
Apply now to my cold dead nose.
Legs akimbo, fist held high,
Tongue stuck out and staring eye,
Thus prepared, you've done your best,
Rigor mortis do the rest.

Off to London take me now,
Bus or train, I care not how,
Grieve ye not, friends, be ye hearty,
Central Office, Tory Party.
Have there, prepared and free from fault,
A medieval catapult,
Primed and ready, waiting there
To propel me through the air.

Now, tory types, my friends tell me,
Like a biscuit with their tea.
Fingers crooked, they quietly sup,
Yes, I'd love another cup.
What the bloody hell is that?
Scalding tea spilled in their laps
As crashing through the window glass,
This present from the working class.

Now through that window as I fly,
Glass and splinters mind not I,
If shattered like that glass will be
Their smug myopic dignity.
If but one moment they regret
A single life that they have wrecked,
Then this one working chap at least
Can lay him down and rest in peace.

Sung to the tune of 'See Amid the Winter's Snow'.

Volunteers welcome.

Galicia

On Galicia's western shore
Where small boats bounce
Effortlessly,
Like spent corks on a restless sea,
There I stayed a while to breathe
And lived and thrived
Contentedly,
By harbour wall and crabby quay.

Where unseen clocks forget the time
And hot dogs languish
Lazily,
In cool shade, one eye to peep,
And the long days slip so slowly by
Through hot afternoons, then,
Seamlessly,
Into jasmine nights and scented sleep.

Beneath my window soft waves stroke
The sighing shore,
Tenderly,
Like loving fingers through pillowed hair,
And so my absent lover's breath
Comes back to me,
Dreamily,
Upon the cool and salty air.

Till morning sun brings fresh delights,
Small kittens curled up
Cosily
Among Geraniums in red clay pots,
While I sit on the step and watch the day
Wake up before me,
Gently;
Today may well be very hot.

Then comes fresh bread in crusty sticks,
Hot blousy armfuls,
Deliciously,
Its sweet aroma calling me
To timeless breakfast by the shore,
Where I watch the day unfold,
Peacefully,
And the small boats heading out to sea.

Soon, the *gaita* calls upon the wind*
With the reeling gulls,
Rhythmically,
Around the hillsides, here and there,
Fiesta time, eat, drink and sing,
Young people dancing without a care,
Happily,
Love, like honeysuckle in the air.

Then, sometimes, on a summer's day,
Things can change,
Suddenly,
For cold mists ride these changing tides.
Silently, they steal ashore
And fishermen may lose their way,
Unexpectedly,
Amid the shrouded headlands and hillsides.

Today, in my mind's eye and in my soul,
Those small boats still bounce,
Endlessly,
In the still, safe harbour of my being,
And the gaita still calls me on the breeze,
Plays to the beating of my heart
Magically,
Beyond the sad horizons of mere seeing.

Gaita: Galician bagpipe.

Shit Happens

Shit happens,
Nose hair grows,
The sun comes up then down she goes,
That's just the way the story goes
And no use in complaining.
We're young too early, wise too late,
Hair deserts the balding pate
But grows like weeds on your best mate,
It's always bloody raining.

But shit happens, life's a hill.
Roll the boulder all you will,
It keeps on rolling back until
It does your bloody brain in.
Bread and jam falls jam-side-down,
Things forgotten come back round,
Wipe away that gloomy frown.
Don't give yourself a caning.

'Cos shit happens, there it is!
No use getting in a tizz
If love seems to have lost its fizz
And your pretty moon is waning.
Hamsters die, lovers leave us,
Heroes fail and friends deceive us.
Life, at times, can be quite grievous,
And often very draining!

But shit happens, end of story!
So it's not all hunky dory.
So your children voted tory,
Sucks to all your training!
In the end you did your best,
Worked your socks off like the rest,
Never mind that life's a mess
And all that weight you're gaining.

Cos shit happens, welcome friend.
Stop pining for that rainbow's end;
It's right there in your heart.
The end.

Ping-pong

So, what do I do now? Ping-pong!
I told myself I'd never share
My heart like this again, but there
You were, that sunset, the balmy air,
And it all went wrong.

What if it's love again... Ding-dong!
That I'm not so tough, not so brave,
And these crazy feelings that I have
Are only, deep down, what I've yearned for
All along!

I must be strong again… King-Kong!
I can take it! Who needs love?
A man like me should be above
Such things. The head can govern
The heart – surely?
Wrong!

There goes my heart again… Sing-song!
Drawn into your nuzzle-night,
A moth toward your gentle light,
Your Icarus, the power for flight
All but gone.

And now the fool again… Ying-tong!
Writing silly verse like this,
Dreaming of your next sweet kiss,
While every empty moment missed
Seems oh so long.

For Maggie, Galicia Oct 1998.

Missing You

I miss you,
too much to carry on
regardless,
too little to call you,
lonely,
in the small, empty hours,
too often to be still,
too infrequently to
give up eating altogether.

There's the problem, you see;
If I loved you too much I'd
damned well get a grip,
too little and I'd find some distraction.
But this crazy happysad,
missyouglad,
kind of wantyoubad
churning inside me
is turning my life
upside down…

Or is it downside up…
maybe outside in?
Who knows…
my head is in
such a spin!

Old Dog

A dog is a dog, is a dog, is a dog,
So some would have us think,
But you, my friend, are a bag of fleas
And you don't half bloody stink.

Your coat's like some mangy, festering rug,
You've been rolling in dog manure,
And, for those who can venture close enough,
Your breath smells like a sewer.

Your eyes are yellow, your teeth are brown,
And your legs are as bandy as hell.
A vet might do something about that arse
If it weren't for the terrible smell.

You're probably deaf, you're surely half-blind,
You're daft as a brush, and you're lazy.
You can hardly be bothered to cock your leg
And your memory's more than hazy.

Your owners have thrown you out in the street,
The kids simply won't go near you,
And she with the fine-groomed pedigree pup
Has every good reason to fear you.

But somebody loves you, sure enough,
For down there, a few dozen paces,
Is a fine young bitch with six young pups
With those same lugubrious faces.

Somebody loves you, mangy old dog,
Well, somebody loves me too,
But I don't think that I'll be taking much
By way of advice from you.

This was a truly disgusting animal that hung around near the house of a friend in Galicia, and is worth immortalising in verse for that reason alone.

Sky

The sky is a vast and silent place,
Those star-specked depths of endless space,
And yet from there I hear your voice,
In each bright star I see your face.

If only you were with me now,
Instead of under distant skies,
Then I would gaze upon your face
And look once more into those eyes

And hold you, beg you not to leave,
Stay with me but one more day,
So I could love you with such words
You could not bear to go away.

Yet still I thank the stars that I
Had you to hold and you to kiss,
For, though you may be far away,
I still have you, my love, to miss.

Hanging On

Like a solitary autumn leaf,
Shimmering on a far-off twig,
your thin and fragile fading form
looks back upon her summer days;
dancing dainty in the breeze,
dancing like a little girl,
all alone in flowery meadows,
stepping like a butterfly,
delicate on girly feet,
crumpled in your wheelie chair.

Now, like gold, the light shines through you,
See your veins against the sky,
glowing in those outer reaches,
twinkling in those soft sky breezes,
whispering your winter song,
whispering like you have a secret,
something special, *'Closer, closer!*
Hear the wind, it tells my story.
Hush, the ages, can't you hear them?'
Dribbling like an infant there.

The ancient oak of generations
holds you gently, proudly, high
among her sighing twigs and branches,
holds you like a tiny baby,
holds you up for all her daughters,
holds you to the white clouds gathering,
bubbling, their feathery billow

white as milk of human kindness,
flecked with birds, each one a story,
like the cake crumbs in your hair.

Time ticks by, another day gone;
sun and cloud like any other.
Touch your paper cheek and, winking,
kiss the button of your nose.
I, your son, shall be your mother,
you with feet in two millennia,
you with feet in zip-up slippers,
egg stains on your lilac cardy,
I shall join you flying daily,
flying in your wheelie chair.

I wrote this for my mother, Ellen Blake, who died in 2007 aged 87. She was a simple soul, in the best sense of that word, but she held our family together through terrible adversity and in spite of my father and his difficult ways.

He Handed Me a Poem

He handed me a poem,
a treasured morsel
of a love that never was,
neat words formed
into a perfect square
in the very centre
of a blank, white, page,
perfectly positioned,
perfectly poised,
polished and justified,
so very neat, like the man,
so utterly formulaic.

A fragment of a person,
suspended briefly
in a moment,
a mere droplet of time,
a short gasp of being,
during which love, let loose,
ran barefoot through gurgling streams
and played in the warm sun
under the head's always watchful,
ever-persecutory gaze.

And the poem, like the man,
played its part to perfection;
a cool, thin masquerade
masking the chaos and the howls,
the screams and the agonies
of stifled love beneath
its swelling page,
a heart bulging like loves breast
through all the calculations -
as love always will –
and always
so perfectly justified.

The Winding Road

One life, so full of twists and turns,
Where does a fellow start?
The trials of the flesh?
The hungry mind?
The pain of a broken heart?
Yet worst of all, as I reflect,
Begins with a lowly birth,
The constant struggle and ceaseless toil
To recognise your worth.

Privilege rests easily
Upon the well-to-do,
And confidence flows freely
When life's been good to you,
But misery and the arse of life
Was mostly what I knew.

Bananas

Is a banana a sausage?
And do two ripe plums make a pear?
Someone I'm sure knows the answer,
Though, frankly, I don't really care.

It's not that philosophy's humdrum,
And I really do love a good riddle,
But, with two sides to every conundrum,
I just slip down the hole in the middle.

Is a banana a sausage,
Or is this some elaborate game?
It can be whatever you want it to be
But the world goes around just the same!

Perhaps it's a question of purpose
And the fate that each has in store,
For the one is a must on the barbie
While the other is best eaten raw.

Is a banana a sausage?
It's not such a ludicrous question,
For the former I'll eat with great gusto,
While the latter gives me indigestion.

Perhaps there is no straight answer,
In spite of their similar features,
But, not being great on philosophy,
I'll concede to the Kants and the Nietzsches.

Worm

They said it would be easy
To decapitate the worm,
One quick chop with a good sharp knife,
Watch it wriggle and squirm,

The whole point being that, in a while,
The absence of a head,
Now lopped off, would render
The little bugger dead.

Imagine their surprise then,
The gruesome business done,
When the tail end of their victim
Simply grew another one.

They were stunned of course, for sure,
Yet, not to be deterred,
They took their knife and lopped its tail,
Fodder for the birds.

Silly, for they should have known!
Imagine their amazement
When the hapless head succeeded
In growing a replacement.

Me, I live and let live,
Eschew all decapitation,
For killing can be no solution
To life's sheer determination.

Written in 2003 at the time of the UK/US moves to 'decapitate' the Iraqi regime by force and to end Saddam Hussein's admittedly tyrannical rule.

Buridan's Ass

Buridan's ass sat in between
Two perfectly sumptuous dinners,
Two equidistant banquets of hay,
But he just couldn't choose so, day after day,
He just sat there getting thinner and thinner.

In truth he was older than Buridan claims
And was well-known to old Aristotle.
But still, day after day, he just sat there and stared
At the two wondrous piles of identical fare,
While his mind raced away at full-throttle.

The puzzle perplexed him, what should he do?
There was no way of making his mind up!
For which pile to choose, there was no way of knowing,
As in coming for one he would also be going…
Surely the ultimate wind-up!

So he sat and he stared, and he thought and he puzzled
But still he could find no basis
For ignoring the first and choosing the second,
For the moment he did then the other one beckoned;
To win was to lose in both cases!

Now perhaps it is so that nothing occurs
Without reason, as Buridan said,
But to place a poor ass in this dire situation,
Where desire of itself leads to certain starvation,
Leads me to conclude – with some indignation –
That he must have been clean off his head.

See-through Glasses

He wore see-through glasses
And through his cidered gaze
He revealed the lives of the see-through men
With their fine un-cidered ways.
Their fine words and reputations,
Their arrogance, their class,
And paper qualifications,
He would use to wipe his arse.

True he weathered badly
And drunk away his sight,
But it never stopped him seeing through
The solid wall of shite
That other men constructed
Around their little lives
Their property, their wealth, their airs,
And their finely-turned-out wives.

A lover of good fiction,
He kept it in its place,
And embraced the contradictions
Of this world we have to face,
A world of greed and opulence,
And of starving babies' cries
That mean nothing to the fat-cats
With their pale unseeing eyes.

He saw the men who pull the strings
For what they really were,
The self-congratulatory scum
Who would have us all defer
To their vision of a 'better world'
(For all that that is worth),
While they send us off to fight their wars
And mutilate the earth.

Cantankerous he may have been,
For he always spoke his mind,
And if he didn't get it right,
His heart was always kind.
Which of course is why we loved him
And excused his errant ways,
While in return he loved full-on
And enriched our waking days.

In fond memory of Jimmy Kerr 1942-2003, a wonderful friend who could be both inspiring and bloody difficult, especially when the drink took him. But no-one could quite cut the crap like he, and he was never one to mince his words.

I wrote this for his funeral and dedicate it to his two daughters, Jane, and Abby (sadly no longer with us) and for Rosalie and Scarlett, his lovely granddaughters of whom he would have been so incredibly proud.

Spyder, Spyder

Spyder! Spyder!
Ghastly fright!
Lurking there by day and night.
What in Heaven or Earth could be
Behind that dreadful symmetry?

From what dark and twisted mind
Did you emerge to scare mankind?
From what tortured madman's pangs
Those scuttling legs, those poison fangs?

Whose bizarre and fiendish art
Created you and stopped my heart,
Then, when my heart screamed out to beat,
To race away on eight swift feet.

Where's my slipper? Where's that stick?
I'll fix you, and fix you quick!
Under which chair did you dart,
Oh terror of my pounding heart?

And when at last I found its lair,
Did I feel guilty? Did I care?
Almost laughing with relief
I crushed it like a dried up leaf.

Spyder! Spyder! Come no more
Scurrying about my floor,
Where no immortal, hand or eye
Protects or gives you sanctuary.

Note that no spiders were harmed in the writing of this poem, even though they still make me shudder, especially those enormous hairy ones that lurk and scuttle around the house.

Sadly, my adult and more nuanced thoughts on the sanctity of life fail me completely, if temporarily, when they take me by surprise like this.

Il Italiano

He, a handsome Italian,
She, a housewife from Wapping.
Her name, Margaret O'Malley,
And she'd stopped for a coffee while out shopping.

She noticed him as he pulled up a chair
Almost opposite her at the table
And she tried so very hard not to stare…
Tried, but was hardly able.

And in that moment she lost her heart,
Her eyes from her head were popping,
He, an Italian, handsome and smart,
She, a housewife from Wapping.

He sipped at his coffee and very soon
He noticed her eyes gazing wide.
'Buongiorno,' he smiled, replacing his spoon,
'Hello,' she meekly replied.

'My name is Dario,' he told her,
'Margaret,' she said with a splutter.
Oh how she wished he would hold her
For her heart was melting like butter.

And as she gazed she fell apart,
Kicking over her bag of shopping.
He an Italian with a smile like the sun,
She, a housewife from Wapping.

When he came to her side to assist her,
His face came so close to hers,
She almost begged him to kiss her,
Her insides were all in a whirr.

And she thought as they quietly chatted,
His voice so soft, so lyrical,
That if he escaped with his trousers intact
It would be little short of a miracle.

She knew now she wanted him, right there and then,
That soon there would be no stopping,
He, an Italian, a god among men,
She a housewife from Wapping.

Across the table they fell in love
While they talked of their dreams and of life.
Then, like a thunderbolt from above,
He asked her to be his wife.

'You come with me to Italy,' he said,
'We live and make love in Milano.
You teach me to make your Toad in the Hole,
I teach you Italiano.'

Oh how she wanted to fall into his arms,
Though the scales from her eyes were now dropping;
He an Italian, single and free,
She, a housewife from Wapping.

'What of my husband?' she thought to herself,
'I can't just run off and leave him.
And what of the children? Though I love this man,
Am I sure that I can believe him?'

So before she left she made him a promise
To love him for a year and a day
And, if after that time, they still felt the same,
Then she'd follow her heart and away.

Oh how she wanted it all to come true.
Oh how her heart was hopping.
He, an Italian, loves dream come true,
She, a housewife from Wapping.

Sparrow

I held you soft in two cupped hands,
as light as smoke,
as transient as a thought,
trembling,
too weak to move,
too exhausted to chirrup,
you stared back at me
barely breathing.

Yet in your lentil eye,
fixed hard on mine,
I saw the tiniest glimmer of hope
as I gazed back down into
the deep, dark well
of life itself.

Pond

Push the fork deep into the earth,
As far as the sole of my shoe,
Wiggle the handle back and forth,
Loosen the unwilling clod,
Lever the handle downwards
Towards me,
Break up that hot grey soil,
Chop up and shovel the dry results
Into the barrow, then
Hard up the plank
And onto the heap
Once more.

Choking dust!
Sore, sweating hands!
Stiff aching back!
Rest.

And… repeat.

Yet, all in good time,
Something resembling
A pond begins to appear,
Nothing from something,
Amazing, like magic,
My own creation emerges
Out of the sun-baked clay,
Kidney-shaped, knee deep,
A whole new world
In waiting, just for me.

Then, under a sweltering sun,
I watch while it crumbles back in,
Like moon dust, back down into the hole.
Shovel it back out again,
Almost as fast as I dare to go,
More and still more,
And still there's more,

Carry on…
Carry on.

For one day, I know, I shall sit and enjoy
The results of my hours of labour.
On some warm summer's evening,
Content, by my pond,
A cold drink in my hand
And a smile on my face,
Along with the clambering frogs,
I shall choose for myself
One frog in particular,
And name the sweet creature
Sisyphus.

We had two apple trees. The one that stood on this spot was half-rotten through and rapidly becoming more wasp than tree. Eventually it could hardly support itself and had to go. In the hole that remained we decided to build a pond –though ' build ' seems a curious word to use in this context.

In the summer of 2018 and in temperatures of well over 30 degrees, I dug out a decent-sized hole. It is now a well-established pond, a haven for wild life, and a delight to sit by on a warm sunny afternoon with a glass of cold white wine.

Sonnet to a Minor Stroke

My right hand wanders off like a puppy dog,
Heedless to my bidding, *Come back here!*
But my will fails me, my mind is fog,
And my wayward puppy has other ideas,
Scatters my brain like a flock of finches,
Fluttering, fearful, in frantic flight.
I try to move but in faltering inches,
Left foot forward, I drag the right.

Something is wrong, I tell my wife,
Dribbled words that make little sense,
But as I fumble, her eyes cry *life,*
Knowing, urgent, her expression tense.
And while my life may teeter on the edge of a knife,
I am trapped in an eternal moment of suspense.

Alive and Creaking

The problem with life,
The only certainty really,
Is that we know it is going to
End badly.

This much said,
The most difficult task ahead,
For me anyway,
Is not to let what I know
Of my ultimate fate
Ruin the time that remains.

Denial is no solution
But nor is delusion
For no god or devil
Awaits us.
After-life and pre-conception,
These are but one and the
Same place, of which
Nothing may be known and
From which
No postcards come home;
No you, no me,
No past, no future.
No time in which
To dwell on regrets.

So praise be for jam today!
Jam for us all!
Is what I say,
And extra for the needy.
Party while you may.
Turn up the music,
And don't mind the neighbours;
Invite them along too.

Only our children and, perhaps,
The pet parrot
Will see
The party out.
For time is on their side,
Not ours.

An Autumn Muse

Autumn arrives,
Summer grown old,
The sun still warm,
The wind turned cold.

Leaves fall like confetti,
Too soon! Too soon!
Winter too soon will
Arrive and take hold.

Last Words to a Dear Friend

Go gently now into that long, kindly night,
So great your pain, so hard your fight,
For just as the flowers and the birds arise
To adorn and sing Spring's early light,
The cycle of life and its changing skies,
They live for their season
And, deep in their being,
They too know when the time is right.

As Spring through your picture window smiles,
Knows all there is of life's rocky miles,
We who have shared your journey sit
And hold your tiny hand a while.
Love, we know, is not just to hold,
Not just to cling to, be it need, be it fear,
Love too must embrace a time for release,
As night follows day on life's spinning dial.

Your eyes are so tired now, so near the end.
Your broken body tried but could not mend,
And we who love you stay with you now;
Gently, in your own time, my lovely friend.
Like the flowers of Spring, you brightened our days,
And fought so hard when the storm clouds rolled in,
But your battle was lost, and the fighting now done,
Little remains for you to defend.

As with such sadness we face
the parting of our ways,
Know you are loved, special friend,
Completely and always.

For Chrissie Mayhew, 7 Feb 2020. The loveliest of friends who finally left us after a long fight with cancer.

February, Somewhere in the North of England or The Discontent of My Winter

I hate winter –
It drags on for far too long:
The cold and the bitter wind of it;
The long and the endless dark of it;
The bare trees and the mud and the rain
As I walk in the park of it;
The never-ending, pouring rain;
The driech and the damp and the drear of it;
The splish and the splosh and the sog of it,
While I look through the window pane
And stand and stare agog at it;
The drizzle and the sleet and the slush and the snow
And the cold impenetrable fog of it;
The freezing fingers, the cold, numb toes,
The stinging ears and the runny nose
As I bravely walk the dog in it;
Gone now the Lycra-lovelies
Who can no longer bear to jog in it;
The nothing-in-the-garden-grows,
The brown-and-sticky-bog of it;
The wellies by the kitchen door,
The thick-caked mud and the clog of it;

The constant struggle to keep myself warm
And the dead-horse-that-I-flog of it
As I curl up by the spluttering stove
And throw another log on it;
The nights, so long, so dark, so cold,
The early-off-to-bed of it,

With its heavy winter duvet,
All thirty seven tog of it,
That I pull up tightly round me,
The inconsiderate hog of it,
Miserably waiting for that distant day,
Still so very far away,
When I no longer need to stay
Curled up indoors and tucked away
From the endless cold, the cheerless grey,
The sheer unrelenting slog of it.

Continuing on the theme of my hatred of winter, this poem, for me, says all that needs to be said. Some of us look to the onset of winter with gloom and foreboding, while others not so afflicted seem to find this impossible to understand and talk of the delight of cold, bright, frosty mornings. I simply cannot get this!

'Nesh' they call it here in Nottingham and I dedicate this to all those others who, like me, have struggled against the odds and against the incredulity of others to put this into words.

A Day Called Night

Out there, a feeble sun is trying to shine,
Or maybe the clouds are trying to prevent it,
Be as it may?
Right now I have little inclination
For nuance or equivocation.
This cold north-easterly warns me
Against previous optimism
And I turn up the heating a notch.
In here, the long day is all mine.

Out there, even the flowers look cold,
Shivering, or is it dancing, trying to keep warm.
Either way!
Right now I see no reason for me
To venture outside to look and see.
While Spring remains stubbornly coiled
And summer holds no fair promise of release,
A bleaker winter now empties the streets,
Laying low the vulnerable and the old.

Out there, the equinox; new hope, new light,
A time to sing and to dance away the dark…
So they say!
Right now it is hard to believe
That winter's blast will ever leave.
As the clocks step forward so we step back,
Back into the shadows, down like moles,
Cower away in our safe dark holes.
Eschew the day and its dubious delights.

Out there, masked faces tense into the wind;
Present tense? Future tense?
Come what may,
Right now, all that each of us can do
Is to carry on, each day anew.
Amid the bloat and the bumble from on high,
The sad lives laid waste in the quest for life,
And the fear behind the mirror's eyes,
We muster what reassurance we can find.

Written during the early days of Lockdown, in fact on the equinox, 21 March 2020. It was terribly cold and bleak and I suffer from chronic asthma so now there were three extremely good reasons for me not to venture outside.

Omicron

It swallowed me like a sea of mud,
Like drowning,
In a deep dark hole,
Alternately boiled and froze my blood,
Woozled my head and sapped my soul.

Aching all over like a beaten rug,
My nose and throat
Are rasped and stung –
While I wallow in a putrid fug –
By the jellyfish swimming in my lungs.

But torment once more gives way to sleep,
As I writhe
And I wriggle
My slow way back,
More a bed now, less a griddle,
The sun rises over my homeward track.

All in a Jumblie

With due credit and greatest respect to Edward Lear.

He took us to sea in a Sieve, he did,
In a Sieve he took us to sea:
In spite of all that we could say,
On a cold winter's morn, on a stormy day,
In a Sieve he took us to sea!
And when the Sieve turned round and round,
And every one cried, 'We'll all be drowned!'
He called aloud, 'Our Sieve ain't big,
But we don't care a button! we don't care a fig!
In a Sieve we'll go to sea!'

Far away, far away
From the lands where the Jumblies live;
He said they were green and their hands were blue,
So we set off to sea in a Sieve.

He sailed us away in a Sieve, he did,
In a Sieve he took us so fast,
With only a dark-blue bigot's scarf,
Tied with a riband by way of a sail,
To a small tobacco-pipe mast;
And every one said, who saw us go,
'O won't they be soon upset, you know!
For the sky is dark, and the voyage is long,
And happen what may, it's extremely wrong
In a Sieve to sail so fast!'

Far away, far away
From the lands where the Jumblies live;
He said they were green and their hands were blue,
So we set off to sea in a Sieve.

The water it soon came in, it did, The water so quickly came in;
So to keep them dry, we wrapped our feet
In a right-wing tabloid, all folded neat,
And we fastened it down with a pin.
And we passed the night in a crockery-jar,
And some still said, 'How wise we are!
Though the sky be dark, and the voyage be long,
Yet we never can think we were rash or wrong,
While round in our sieve we spin!'

Far away, far away
From the lands where the Jumblies live;
He said they were green and their hands were blue,
So we set off to sea in a Sieve.

And all night long we sailed away;
And when the sun went down,
He whistled and warbled a rousing song
To the echoing sound of an American gong,
In the shade of the mountains brown.
'O Timballo! How happy we are,
When we live in a Sieve and a crockery-jar,
And all night long in the moonlight pale,
We sail away with our dark-blue sail,
In the shade of the mountains brown!'

Far away, far away
From the lands where the Jumblies live;
He said they were green and their hands were blue,
So we set off to sea in a Sieve.

He sailed us to far off lands, he did,
Where the markets were fair and free,
And we bought an Owl, and a useful Cart,
And a pound of Rice, and a Cranberry Tart,
And a hive of half-alive bees.
And we bought a Pig, and some green Jack-daws,
And a lovely Monkey with lollipop paws,
And forty bottles of Ring-Bo-Ree,
And we lived on Stilton Cheese.

Far away, far away
From the lands where the Jumblies live;
He said they were green and their hands were blue,
So we set off to sea in a Sieve.

And in twenty years we all wanted back,
In twenty years or more,
And every one said, 'How poor they've grown!
For they've been to the Lakes, and the Torrible Zone,
And the hills of the Chankly Bore!'
Where they drank too much and did greatly feast
And they cursed the grumbly eurobeast;
And every one said, 'If we only live,
We will never go to sea in a Sieve,
To the hills of the Chankly Bore!'

Far away, far away
From the lands where the Jumblies live;
He said they were green and their hands were blue,
So we set off to sea in a Sieve.

Early Spring 2020, on the event of the UK leaving the European Union and just before Covid lockdown. Lear's flair for absurdity was an irresistible temptation in these ill-advised and depressing circumstances.

Letter to Santa

Dear Santa,
Please will you bring me a gun,
Not just a toy
One though;
A proper one,

All shiny and silver,
That spits real fire
And shoots real bullets.
I'll be a 'Gun for Hire'

And I'll kill all the baddies
And that Spencer Street lot
And that Mickey McIver
Who won't take his shots
And my big sister
Who's always picking on me
And I'll be like a sniper
And wait in a tree
And I'll pick off the lot of them,
One…two…three,
And then,
When I've done all that,
We'll go home for our tea.

Dear Santa,
Please will you bring back my son.
He wasn't a bad lad,
Honestly he wasn't;
He was so kind and full of fun.

But the stories he heard,
They turned his young head,
And he turned to the gangs
On the street instead.

And they talked about fast cars
And quick, easy cash,
And quick, easy girls,
And their coke and their hash,
And they played their loud music
With faces like stone,
In the corners and shadows
Where they'd be left alone.
But the cool they exuded
Froze them down to the bone
And they shot
My lovely boy
For his expensive new phone.

Dear Santa
Please rid us of all these guns,
For the sake of all
Our lovely
Daughters and sons.

For ignorant men
Have filled our son's heads
With tales of glory
On the backs of the dead,
In a world that revolves
Around profit and greed
With no thought for the pain
Of those so greatly in need,

And no heed to the grief,
The misery, the damage,
The hunger and the death,
And the wreckage and carnage.
Santa please save us,
From our terrible plight.
Please, please bring us peace
And love in abundance
This Christmas Night.

Girly Swat

Dear Boris Johnson,

Perhaps I was a 'girly swat'
When I was still at school,
But I learned things that you did not,
Yours, the dunce's stool.

Now you're just a bumbling clot
Who thinks he's born to rule,
While stoking up the rich man's lot,
Filthy Lucre's fool.

On Growing Old

Growing old is not so bad –
Not so *good*, mind –
But not so bad.
And consider this, should you find you hunger
For good times past and those you've lost,
This only means that you didn't die younger,
Old age being the inevitable cost.

Growing old can be quite fun –
Hardly *hilarious*, mind –
But, still, quite fun.
And while our bodies may cease to flatter,
Such things we take less seriously,
Our sense of proportion being more what matters,
Our love, our experience, our empathy.

Grandchildren can be best of all –
Not *all* the time, mind –
But, still, best of all.
They'll have us in stitches or reduce us to tears,
And pay little heed to the things that we teach,
While shoving Weetabix in their ears
And any orifice within easy reach.

Growing old's not really so bad –
It can be, mind –
But it's mostly not bad.
Sure, I grow daily more dotty, it seems,
While my hip and my knees and my back give me gip,
And I struggle with memories, now, rather than dreams,
But I still have my humour –
Did I mention my hip?

The inspiration for the following poem came from a reading of the Chilean poet, Gabriela Mistral, more specifically, her poem Besos (Kisses).

To the Wind a Seed

Was it given, or was it stolen?
Did I bring or did I take away?
Whose the loss and whose the gain?
All I know for sure is this,
That I dissolved with that first kiss,
And would never be the same again.

Was it love or was it need,
Curiosity, perhaps, or desire?
These things will not be teased apart,
For the softness of your lips that day,
Your look that never went away,
Live on to this day in my heart.

And yet, in truth, she will never know,
For what flower, once its seeds are cast,
Reflects on where they land at last
Or how beautiful they just might grow.

Nuggets of Gold

Locked down in these long days of isolation,
I feels as though I am growing old
For I have so much time to sit and ponder
Both the mud of life and its nuggets of gold.

Here, tucked away in the creases of time,
There are diamonds to be found for the keener eye,
Things that force us to stop in wonder,
Things that could so easily pass us by.

For the moment is truly a special thing,
So easily missed in the clamour to find
Those future moments, to seek and then squander,
To assuage and to gorge the unquiet mind.

And I stop and I ask myself, what are our years,
So many flown past in a life's long haul,
If not those same precious moments
Writ large, writ fonder,
Nuggets of gold to cherish and recall.

For Little Arthur

Little Arthur died today.
Poisoned, beaten, kicked and neglected,
His woeful cries for food rejected,
He sobbed his loveless life away.

It seemed the whole world stopped right there
As people wept and hugged each other,
Speechless at his cruel stepmother,
Anger mixed with pure despair.

Little Arthur, what can we say?
Your pitiful screams went by unheard,
Your suffering, way beyond mere words.
But your memory will never go away
For something died in us all today.

Little Arthur Labinjo-Hughes died appallingly at the hands of his father and stepmother on 17 June 2020 in Solihull. Much of his dreadful suffering was preserved on over 200 recordings on the family's CCTV camera and shocked everyone beyond belief.

From the very beginning he was a child without hope: his actual mother, Olivia Labinjo-Halcrow, 27, was in jail for stabbing her own partner to death in a drink and drug-fuelled rage.

Villanelle for an Ageing Socialist

Little by little, day by day,
the mirror tells us we grow frail and old,
yet still we refuse to fade away.

Still we struggle as best we may,
To keep up the fight, determined and bold,
bit by bit, day by day.

More needy ourselves now, still we say
that our love and our passion will never grow cold,
our principles never fade away.

And though the hounds of war may bay
and the schemes of crazy men unfold,
to threaten this world and destroy our days,

And while bloated fat-cats feast and play
on the backs of the needy and the old,
we refuse to lie down or fade away.

We may be forgetful, we may be grey,
and we may shake now that we are old,
but we know there is a far better way.
Do not imagine we are going away.

Postscript:

>Listen, you young men, to what we say,
>This world will be all yours one day,
>Look after it, don't throw it all away.

To David Jackson.

Seasonal Haikus
Mid-Lockdown, 2020

Christmas is almost
upon us, or so they said.
That was in August.

Then in September
We began to get anxious
Would we miss it all?

October, by now
We were just a bag of nerves
No time left to waste.

Early November
Crowded shops fast selling out.
Frayed nerves. Tempers lost.

Then when Christmas came
We all collapsed at long last.
Too worn out to move.

Not like that this year.
Bubble-wrapped isolation.
A modest affair.

Twenty-Twenty Hindsight

During AD 2020
My cynicism grew aplenty
'Till, by 2021,
So much damage had been done,
I reached the limits of my tether
And gave up counting altogether.

But please don't let me spoil the fun;
Happy New Year Everyone.

By the time 2020 got going many of us felt that the juggernaut of doom was heading our way. Perhaps it was!

Beware the Ignoramus

Beware the ignoramus
Who believes he's worldly wise,
Who cannot see what others see,
Who can't tell truth from lies,
Yet won't believe the evidence
Right there before his eyes.

He's so convinced, he never learns
And never even tries,
And thinks that hard-won learning
Is something to despise,
But, without the power to reason,
From the mud can never rise.

Beware the ignoramus
Who wallows in the mire.
Believing it's the mountain top
And there is nothing higher,
For he cannot tell the wise man
From the scoundrel and the liar.

Beware the ignoramus
Who never seems to tire
Of his diet of rank absurdity,
His bitterness and his ire,
Yet will throw the works of wiser souls
To burn upon his fire.

The germ of this piece came when Donald Trump suggested

vaccinating people with disinfectant as a precaution against Covid.

The Day I Found a Frog in Our Toilet

There's a frog in the toilet, I told her.
Don't be so daft, she said,
But I had to insist, having almost pissed
On top of the poor thing's head.

How fortunate then, that unlike her,
When we chaps go off to the loo,
We've a chance to see, before we pee,
What we are about to do.

Ladies, though, go bottoms-first,
And, true, they don't pee on the floor,
But any poor frog who climbs into that bog
Will get more than it bargained for.

So please take a moment to check
Before you go to the loo,
For you never quite know who sits below,
Staring anxiously back up at you.

Another true story. The frog eventually escaped unscathed the way it had come.

Poetry Read in a Silly Voice

Open the book, select the page,
Assume the look of a world-wise sage,
Prepare your throat, for it should be moist
For poetry, read in a silly voice.

Stand up tall and with dignity,
Fill your lungs to capacity,
Quake those rafters, shake those joists
With your poetry, read in a silly voice.

Be it Shakespeare, be it Yeats,
Auden, Thomas, Elliot or Keats,
Heaney, Shelley , Pam Ayres, or Joyce
Regale them with your silly voice.

Project, project for all you're worth,
To all who live upon this Earth,
May they hear you and rejoice
Your poetry read in a silly voice.

Rage, rage against the trend
To read like a dullard from Southend,
Damn the eyes of those who foist
Their poetry with an Essex voice.

Yours be the glory, yours the prize,
Yours the gleam in Heaven's eye,
For yours has been the noblest choice;
Poetry read in a silly voice.

Not Raving but Clowning

With due credit and great respect to Stevie Smith

No-one paid much attention
To his larking about that morning:
But he went too far, some of them thought,
And it seemed more like raving than clowning.

Poor chap, he loved a good laugh,
But they locked him away without warning.
He was a bit far-out for some people's taste,
So they thought he was raving, not clowning.

But no, oh no, it was always in jest,
Though they treated him something appalling,
And he'd been far-out for most of his life,
Not raving at all, but clowning.

A 'Real Man' Declares his Love

If I loved you more than this,
I don't think I could bear it.
If that makes me a soppy shite,
Well, I don't mind, perhaps they're right –
The cap fits, I must wear it.

Thingummyjig

Now that I'm old it's such a shame,
I can't remember my own name.
Perhaps it's Fred, or maybe Joe,
Truth is, I no longer know!
What am I supposed to do
When the mirror asks me, *Who are you?*

They tied a label round my neck
But that for me was too hi-tech.,
All that paper, all that string,
And words that didn't mean a thing.

So then my wife, *What's 'ername*,
To my rescue kindly came,
And wrote it down with marker pen
Upon my hand, and then again,
Upon the other, knowing I might
Forget my left hand from my right.
Yet still I have no memory
Of whose name this is meant to be
And struggle on, never knowing,
Who I am or where I'm going.

So now, my memory almost gone,
I sign this poem off…

Anon

A concluding word on the importance of maintaining a sense of humour and fun, even during difficult times.

About the Author

Vic Blake was born in May 1947 in the London Borough of Fulham, soon after the end of the Second World War. These were extremely austere and difficult times, with very little money to go round and with post-war rationing creating severe shortages. Living in a cold, damp basement, the whole family suffered with serious ill-health. Vic, himself, spent much of his early years in hospital or in convalescent homes, and later in special, open-air schools for children of a 'delicate' disposition. These experiences turned out to have a considerable effect on his life.

At the age of twelve his family moved away from London to Hertfordshire, where the air was cleaner, but where he left school, aged fifteen, with no recognisable qualifications. After holding down a series of unskilled and semi-skilled jobs, he joined the army, partly because he needed to break away, but mostly to escape from an impossibly difficult father.

Later, having left the army somewhat prematurely, He drifted for a while, working here and there and travelling around Europe and Morocco before eventually enrolling at college and training and settling down as a teacher. He went on to complete his Masters' degree in 1984 but then, while doing background research for a PhD, he was hit by an oncoming car, leaving him seriously injured, partially disabled and in constant pain. The PhD never happened.

Nearly a decade later, still troubled by pain and now losing his hearing, he took early retirement from teaching and began a three-year course in counselling and psychotherapy. Being a committed profeminist, he quickly developed a keen interest in working with men and this was to open up a whole new world of insight into his own and other men's worlds as well as a new direction in his own life.

But, still affected by chronic pain, he was eventually forced to retire altogether, after which he went to live in Galicia in N.W. Spain, where he continued to research and write on men and masculinity issues. This was to become the main focus of his writing for over twenty years, though recently he turned his hand more seriously to writing fiction.

Vic now lives in Nottingham with his wife Maggie.

Also by Vic Blake:

So anyway… a collection of short stories.
(2020, Oxford eBooks).

vicblake@ntlworld.com
www.vicblakewriter.co.uk

www.ingramcontent.com/pod-product-compliance
Lightning Source LLC
Chambersburg PA
CBHW021154080526
44588CB00008B/325